Presented To The Stockton
Township Public Library

By the
Alice E. Krause
Memorial
2004

THE MAN WHO WALKED BETWEEN THE TOWERS

MORDICAI GERSTEIN

Roaring Brook Press **Brookfield, Connecticut**

TO PHILIPPE PETIT
for the gifts of his courage,
his impeccable art,
and his mythic sense of mischief

ACKNOWLEDGMENT

I often enjoyed Philippe Petit's New York street performances in the 1970s, but regretfully, I did not witness his walk between the towers. My sources for this book were Gwen Kinkead's 1987 NEW YORKER profile of Petit, ALONE AND IN CONTROL; articles and pictures in THE NEW YORK TIMES; THE NEW YORK POST; THE DAILY NEWS; and Petit's own book about his walk, TO REACH THE CLOUDS. Philippe Petit has done many wire walks since the one described here.

Copyright © 2003 by Mordicai Gerstein
Published by Roaring Brook Press
A Division of The Millbrook Press, 2 Old New Milford Road, Brookfield, Connecticut 06804
All rights reserved

Library of Congress Cataloging-in-Publication Data
Gerstein, Mordicai.
The man who walked between the towers / Mordicai Gerstein.—1st ed.
p.   cm.
Summary: A lyrical evocation of Philippe Petit's 1974 tightrope walk between the World Trade Center towers.
1. Petit, Philippe, 1949- —Juvenile literature. 2. Tightrope walking—Juvenile literature.
3. Aerialists—France—Juvenile literature. [1. Petit, Philippe, 1949- 2. Aerialists. 3. Tightrope walking.
4. World Trade Center (New York, NY)] I. Title.
GV551.G47 2003
791.3'4'092—dc21   2003009040

ISBN 0-7613-1791-0 (trade edition)
3 5 7 9 10 8 6 4
ISBN 0-7613-2868-8 (library binding)
3 5 7 9 10 8 6 4 2

Book design by Filomena Tuosto
Printed in the United States of America
First edition

Once there were two towers side by side.
They were each a quarter of a mile high;
one thousand three hundred and forty feet.
The tallest buildings in New York City.

A young man saw them rise into the sky.

He was a street performer. He rode a unicycle.

He juggled balls and fiery torches.

But most of all he loved to walk and dance
on a rope he tied between two trees.

He looked not at the towers but at the space between them
and thought, what a wonderful place to stretch a rope;
a wire on which to walk. Once the idea came to him
he knew he had to do it! If he saw three balls, he had to juggle.
If he saw two towers, he had to walk! That's how he was.

Hadn't he danced on a wire between the steeples of
Notre Dame Cathedral above his amazed home city, Paris?
Why not here, between these towers?

Of course he knew that, as in Paris, the police
and the owners of the towers would never allow it.
You must be crazy! they would say. You'd fall for sure!

And so Philippe—that was the young man's name—
began a plan to do it secretly.
The buildings are not quite finished, he thought.
Maybe if I dressed as a construction worker. . . .

Early on an August evening he and a friend entered the south tower.

They got a four-hundred-and-forty-pound reel of cable and other equipment into the elevator, took it to the unfinished top ten floors, and waited till nightfall when everyone had gone.

Then they carried everything up one hundred and eighty stairs to the roof.

At midnight, on the other tower's roof, two more friends tied a thin, strong line
to an arrow and shot it across to Philippe, one hundred and forty feet away.

It missed, and landed on a ledge fifteen feet below the roof.

Bad luck! thought Philippe.

He crawled down to the ledge, over the sparkling city, and got the arrow.

To its line he tied a stronger line, which his friends pulled back to their tower.

To his end of the stronger line, Philippe tied the cable
on which he would walk. It was seven-eighths of an inch thick.

His friends pulled the cable over to their tower
but it was so heavy that it slipped from Philippe's grip.
The cable's middle plummeted toward the street—

pulling the friends on the other tower
to the very
edge.

Philippe, just in time, secured his end.

It took three hours to pull the cable back up.

Frantically, as the stars faded, they tightened it between the towers.

It was past dawn before they were ready.

Philippe put on his black shirt and tights.

He picked up his twenty-eight-foot balancing pole.

All his life he had worked to be here; to do this.

As the rising sun lit up the towers, out he stepped onto the wire.

Out to the very middle he walked, as if he were walking on the air itself.

Many winds whirled up from between the towers, and he swayed with them.

He could feel the towers breathing.

He was not afraid.

He felt alone and happy and absolutely free.

A woman coming from the subway
might have been the first to see him.
"Look! Someone walking on
a wire between the towers!"

Everyone stopped and looked up.

They gasped and stared.

It was astonishing.

It was terrifying and beautiful.

A quarter of a mile up in the sky

someone was dancing.

Police saw it, too.

Officers rushed to the roofs of the towers.
"You're under arrest!" they shouted through bullhorns.
Philippe turned and walked the other way.

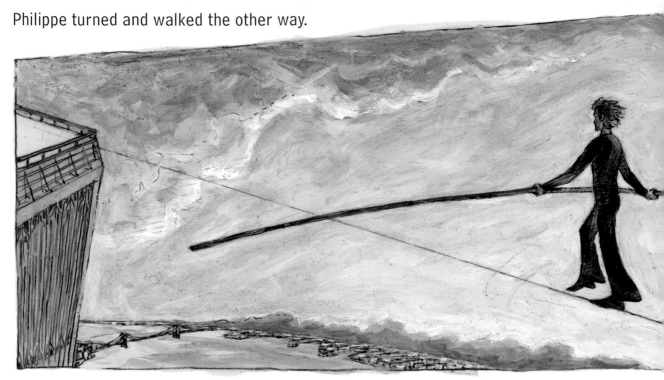

Who would come and get him?

For almost an hour, back and forth,
he walked, danced, ran, and knelt in a salute upon the wire.

He even lay down to rest.
The city and harbor spread beneath him.
The sky surrounded him.
Seagulls flew under and over.
As long as he stayed on the wire
he was free.

When he felt completely satisfied, he walked back to the roof
and held out his wrists for the handcuffs.

They brought him to court. The judge sentenced him
to perform in the park for the children of the city.

This he did happily. . . though during his performance some boys playing
on his wire jerked it and Philippe fell

. . . but caught himself.

Now the towers are gone.

But in memory, as if imprinted on the sky, the towers are still there.
And part of that memory is the joyful morning, August 7, 1974,
when Philippe Petit walked between them in the air.